The Art of Salsa Cooking

Salsa Recipes for You

By

Heston Brown

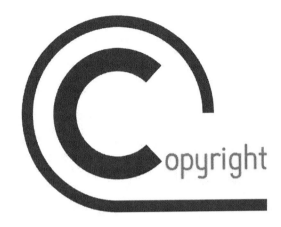

Copyright 2019 Heston Brown

All rights reserved. No part of this Book should be reproduced by any means including but not limited to: digital or mechanical copies, printed copies, scanning or photocopying unless approval is given by the Owner of the Book.

Any suggestions, guidelines or ideas in the Book are purely informative and the Author assumes no responsibility for any burden, loss, or damage caused by a misunderstanding of the information contained therein. The Reader assumes any and all risk when following information contained in the Book.

Thank you so much for buying my book! I want to give you a special gift!

Receive a special gift as a thank you for buying my book. Now you will be able to benefit from free and discounted book offers that are sent directly to your inbox every week.

To subscribe simply fill in the box below with your details and start reaping the rewards! A new deal will arrive every day and reminders will be sent so you never miss out. Fill in the box below to subscribe and get started!

https://heston-brown.getresponsepages.com

Table of Contents

Chapter I - Avocado Salsa Recipes 7

Recipe 1: Mango and Avocado Salsa 8

Recipe 2: Avocado Salsa 10

Recipe 3: Avocado and Grape Salsa 13

Recipe 4: Avocado Salsa with Tortilla 15

Recipe 5: Creamy Salsa with Avocado 18

Recipe 6: Exciting Salsa 20

Chapter II - Salsa Verde Recipes 23

Recipe 7: Morelos Salsa 24

Recipe 8: Mexico Salsa Verde 27

Recipe 9: Tomatillo Salsa 30

Recipe 10: Garlic Salsa with Tomatillo 32

Recipe 11: Salsa Costena 35

Recipe 12: Green Salsa 38

Chapter III - Delicious Tomato Salsa Recipes 40

Recipe 13: Salsa without Onion 41

Recipe 14: Famous Salsa 43

Recipe 15: Spicy Salsa 45

Recipe 16: Jalapeno and Tomato Salsa 47

Recipe 17: Habanero and Tomato Salsa 49

Recipe 18: Mexina Salsa 51

Chapter IV - Delicious Recipes for Corn Salsa 53

Recipe 19: Corn and Tomato Salsa 54

Recipe 20: Pico de Gallo and Corn Salsa 56

Recipe 21: Black Bean Salsa with Corn 59

Recipe 22: Black Bean and Cheese Salsa 61

Recipe 23: Roasted and Chipotle Salsa with Corn 64

Recipe 24: Corn Salad with Cilantro 67

Chapter V - Mango and Peach Salsa Recipes 69

Recipe 25: Chipotle Peach Salsa 70

Recipe 26: Peach Salsa with Cinnamon Chips 72

Recipe 27: Peachanero Salsa 75

Recipe 28: Mango Salsa 77

Recipe 29: Apple and Peach Salsa 79

Recipe 30: Peach and Pineapple Salsa 81

About the Author 84

Author's Afterthoughts 86

Chapter I - Avocado Salsa Recipes

You can enjoy some delicious salsa recipes with avocado, tomato and some fruity combinations. There are some amazing recipes for your help.

xxxxxxxxxxxxxxxxxxxxxxxxxxxxxxxxxxxxxx

Recipe 1: Mango and Avocado Salsa

Cooking Time: 45 minutes

Yield: 6

List of Ingredients:

- Mango (diced, seeded and peeled): 1
- Diced, pitted and peeled avocado: 1
- Tomatoes: 4 medium
- Diced jalapeno pepper (minced and seeded): 1
- Chopped cilantro: half cup
- Minced garlic: 3 pieces
- Chopped onion (red): 1/4 mug
- Salt: one tsp.
- Olive oil: 3 Tbsp.
- Lime juice: 2 Tbsp.

xxxxxxxxxxxxxxxxxxxxxxxxxxxxxxxxxxxxxxx

Instructions:

Take one medium bowl and combine garlic, jalapeno, cilantro, tomatoes, mango and avocado in one bowl. Stir in olive oil, lime juice, red onion, and salt. It will help you to blend all flavors and put them in the fridge for almost 30 minutes. Serve chilled.

Recipe 2: Avocado Salsa

Cooking Time: 25 minutes

Yield: 16

List of Ingredients:

- Red onion (diced): 1 cup
- Avocado (pitted, diced and chopped): 2 cups
- White onion (diced): 1 cup
- Corn kernels: 2 cups
- Salt: 1 1/2 Tbsp.
- Red bell pepper (diced): 1 cup
- Ground cumin: 2 tsp.
- White vinegar: 2 Tbsp.
- Green bell pepper (diced): 1/2 cup
- Olive oil: 1/4 cup
- Black pepper (ground): 2 tsp.
- Red vinegar: 1 tsp.
- Chili powder: 1 tsp.
- Cilantro leaves (chopped): 2 cups
- Diced tomatoes: 1 1/2 cups
- Juiced and zested: 1 lime

xxxxxxxxxxxxxxxxxxxxxxxxxxxxxxxxxxxxxx

Instructions:

Heat oil in one skillet over high flame and cook corn kernel in your hot skillet. Turn frequently to avoid burning. You have to cook for almost five minutes.

Take one mixing bowl and mix corn, chili powder, red vinegar, black pepper, cumin, salt, white vinegar, olive oil, bell pepper (green) and bell pepper (red), white onion, red onion and avocado in this bowl. Add tomatoes, lime juice, lime zest and cilantro to corn mixture and stir gently to incorporate all ingredients.

Recipe 3: Avocado and Grape Salsa

Cooking Time: 50 minutes

Yield: 8

List of Ingredients:

- Chopped red grapes without seeds: 1 1/2 cups
- Diced, peeled and pitted avocado: 1
- Chopped bell pepper in red color: 1/4 cup
- Chopped bell pepper in yellow color: 2 Tbsp.
- Chopped onion: 2 Tbsp.
- Chopped cilantro: 2 Tbsp.
- Lime juice: 1 Tbsp.
- Garlic salt: 1/2 tsp.
- Black pepper (ground): 1 pinch

xxxxxxxxxxxxxxxxxxxxxxxxxxxxxxxxxxx

Instructions:

Put cilantro, onion, yellow pepper, red pepper, avocados and grapes in one bowl. Stir in black pepper, garlic salt, and lime juice. Gently mix all ingredients together to mix them well. Put in your fridge for almost 30 minutes and serve chilled.

Recipe 4: Avocado Salsa with Tortilla

Cooking Time: 30 minutes

Yield: 8

List of Ingredients:

- Diced Avocado (pitted and peeled): 8
- Cherry tomatoes in Yellow Color (quartered): 1/2 cup
- Chopped red onion: 1/4
- Chopped cilantro: 2 Tbsp.
- Jalapeno pepper (seeded and discard membrane): ½
- Chopped pepper: ½
- Ground cardamom: 1/4 tsp.
- Lime (juiced): 1
- Lemon juice: 1 Tbsp.

Chips:

- Flour tortillas (8 wedges): 10 small
- Olive Oil: 1/4 cup
- Cinnamon sugar: 2 Tbsp.

xxxxxxxxxxxxxxxxxxxxxxxxxxxxxxxxxxxxx

Instructions:

Mix jalapeno pepper, cilantro, onion, tomatoes, and avocado in one bowl. Sprinkle with some cardamom and pour lemon juice and lime juice over salsa. Toss well to coat.

Preheat your oven to nearly 350° F.

Carefully brush all tortilla wedges with some olive oil and generously sprinkle with cinnamon sugar. Now arrange all coated wedges on one baking sheet.

Bake in your preheated oven for almost 15 minutes to make chips crispy. You can serve crispy chips with peach salsa.

Recipe 5: Creamy Salsa with Avocado

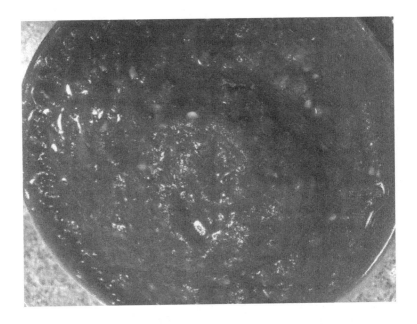

Cooking Time: 1 hour 15 minutes

Yield: 24

List of Ingredients:

- Tomato sauce: 8 ounces
- Water: 1 cup
- Mexican-style tomato hot sauce: 7.75 ounces
- Tomatoes (quartered): 3
- Trimmed onions: 2 green
- Fresh cilantro (trim stems): 1 bunch
- ½-inch pieces of jalapeno pepper (with seeds): 1
- Salt: 1 tsp.
- Diced Avocados: 2
- Diced tomatoes: 2

xxxxxxxxxxxxxxxxxxxxxxxxxxxxxxxxxxxxx

Instructions:

Combine green onions, jalapeno, cilantro, tomatoes, tomato sauce, water, salt and hot sauce in one blender. Blend well to combine for almost 10 – 15 seconds.

Pour this mixture into one bowl and mix in avocados and diced tomatoes. Cover this salsa bowl with plastic and put in your fridge for one hour.

Recipe 6: Exciting Salsa

Cooking Time: 1 hour 20 minutes

Yield: 5

List of Ingredients:

- Olive oil: 1 Tbsp.
- Diced yellow onion: 1
- Diced bell pepper: 1 green
- Chopped garlic: 2 cloves
- Cayenne pepper: 1 1/2 tsp.
- Mashed avocado: 1
- Tomato sauce: 1/2 cup
- Lemon juice: 2 Tbsp.
- Olive oil: 1 Tbsp.
- Ground coriander: 1 Tbsp.
- Fresh cilantro (chopped): 1 Tbsp.

xxxxxxxxxxxxxxxxxxxxxxxxxxxxxxxxxxxxxxx

Instructions:

Heat oil in one skillet over medium flame. Cook garlic, onion and bell pepper in this oil, for almost 5 – 7 minutes. Dust some cayenne pepper over onion mixture and transfer in your bowl. Keep it aside to let this mixture cool.

Toss cilantro, coriander, olive oil, lemon juice, tomato sauce and avocado in one bowl and add onion blend in this bowl. Gently mix all ingredients to combine.

Cover this bowl with plastic cover and put in your fridge for one hour. Serve chilled.

Chapter II - Salsa Verde Recipes

There are some delicious Salsa Verde recipes to entertain your taste buds. You can serve these Verdes with bread, sandwiches and tacos.

xxxxxxxxxxxxxxxxxxxxxxxxxxxxxxxxxxxxxx

Recipe 7: Morelos Salsa

Cooking Time: 30 minutes

Yield: 16

List of Ingredients:

- Tomatillos (husked): 2 pounds
- Jalapeno peppers (fresh): 2
- Peeled garlic: 3 cloves
- Cloves: 1 dash
- Ground cumin: 1/2 tsp.
- Black pepper: 1 dash
- Chicken bouillon (granules): 1 tsp.
- Salt: as per taste

xxxxxxxxxxxxxxxxxxxxxxxxxxxxxxxxxxx

Instructions:

Take one pot and put garlic, jalapeno, and tomatillos in this pot. Pour sufficient water to cover these ingredients. If the tomatillos start floating, press them downward with your hand. Put this pot over high heat to boil and then decrease heat to medium to simmer this mixture for almost 10 minutes. The color of tomatillos will turn into yellow. Turn off heat and let these ingredients cool for nearly 10 minutes

Strain this tomatillos mixture and reserve its water. Put tomatillos in your blender along with chicken bouillon, pepper, cumin and cloves. Puree all ingredients to make them smooth and use reserved water to adjust the consistency of this salsa.

Recipe 8: Mexico Salsa Verde

Cooking Time: 45 minutes

Yield: 40

List of Ingredients:

- Tomatillos (husked & chopped): 12
- Chopped jalapenos (drained): 7 ounces
- Chopped lettuce: 1/2 head
- Chopped garlic: 2 cloves
- Chopped and dried cilantro: 1/3 cup
- Ground cumin: 3 Tbsp.
- Pepper and salt: as per taste
- Butter: 2 Tbsp.
- Chopped onion: ¼
- Chicken broth: 1/4 cup

xxxxxxxxxxxxxxxxxxxxxxxxxxxxxxxxxxxxx

Instructions:

Combine pepper, salt, cumin, cilantro, garlic, lettuce, jalapenos and tomatillos in one food processor or blender and process well to get desired consistency.

Take one saucepan and melt butter over medium flame. Cook onion in melted butter for almost 5 minutes to make them translucent. Pour the chicken broth and tomatillo mixture in saucepan and cook for nearly 20 minutes to make salsa thick. Stir frequently to avoid sticking and burning. After getting desired consistency, turn off heat.

Recipe 9: Tomatillo Salsa

Cooking Time: 30 minutes

Yield: 16

List of Ingredients:

- Tomatillos (husked): 10
- Chopped onion: 1 small
- Chopped garlic: 3 cloves
- Chopped jalapeno peppers: 2
- Chopped cilantro: 1/4 cup
- Pepper and salt: as per taste

xxxxxxxxxxxxxxxxxxxxxxxxxxxxxxxxxxxxx

Instructions:

Take one nonreactive or nonstick saucepan, add tomatillos and fill it with sufficient water to cover tomatillos. Let it boil and simmer for almost 10 minutes to make tomatillos soft.

Drain tomatillos and put in one blender or food processor with pepper, salt, cilantro, jalapeno peppers, garlic, and onion. Blend these ingredients well to get desired consistency.

Recipe 10: Garlic Salsa with Tomatillo

Cooking Time: 40 minutes

Yield: 20

List of Ingredients:

- Fresh tomatillos (remove husks): 1 pound
- Separated garlic cloves (peeled): 1 head
- Jalapeno peppers: 3 fresh
- Fresh cilantro: 1 bunch
- Water: 1/2 cup
- Pepper and salt: as per your taste

XXXXXXXXXXXXXXXXXXXXXXXXXXXXXXXXXXXX

Instructions:

Preheat your oven broiler.

Arrange the jalapenos, tomatillos and whole garlic cloves on one baking sheet. Put these ingredients under preheated broiler and cook them for few minutes. Remove cloves of garlic first after toasting them to avoid bitter flavor.

Continue roasting tomatillos and jalapenos to make them equally charred. Turn occasionally and keep it aside to let them cool. There is no need to remove the overcooked parts of peppers or tomatillos. They will give a unique flavor to your salsa.

Put tomatillos and peppers in one blender along with cilantro and garlic. Add some water to this mixture to blend all ingredients easily. Season with pepper and salt and put in your fridge until serving.

Recipe 11: Salsa Costena

Cooking Time: 45 minutes

Yield: 8

List of Ingredients:

- Chile peppers (costeno Amarillo): 6
- Tomatillos (husked): 1/2 pound
- Garlic: 1 clove
- Chopped onion: 1/2 cup
- Chopped cilantro: 1/3 cup
- Salt: 1/2 tsp.

xxxxxxxxxxxxxxxxxxxxxxxxxxxxxxxxxxxxx

Instructions:

Take one medium skillet and put it over medium flame to heat some oil and cook chile peppers. Stir peppers consistently to make them dark brown. Be careful and don't let peppers to stick or burn. Turn off heat and keep peppers aside.

Put tomatillos in one medium saucepan and cover them with sufficient water. Let this water boil and cook for almost five minutes on medium flame. Turn off heat and drain well.

Place garlic, tomatillos and chile peppers in one food processor or blender and blend these ingredients to make a smooth mixture. Transfer this mixture to one medium bowl and stir in salt, cilantro, and onion. Put in fridge to chill until serving.

Recipe 12: Green Salsa

Cooking Time: 30 minutes

Yield: 20

List of Ingredients:

- Tomatillos (husked and chopped): 2 pounds
- Chopped green tomatoes: 3
- Olive oil: 1/2 cup
- Mild and chopped chile peppers: 2
- Chopped shallot: 1
- Chopped cilantro: 5 sprigs
- White vinegar (distilled): 1/3 cup
- Garlic powder: 1/4 cup
- Salt: 1 tsp.

xxxxxxxxxxxxxxxxxxxxxxxxxxxxxxxxxxxx

Instructions:

Place the tomatoes, tomatillos, oil, salt, garlic powder, vinegar, cilantro, shallots, and chili pepper in one saucepan and cook it over medium heat. Let it boil and then decrease heat to medium and simmer for almost 15 – 20 minutes to make tomatillos soft.

Pour this mixture into the blender and puree to make it smooth. Put in fridge to chill and serve.

Chapter III - Delicious Tomato Salsa Recipes

There are some good salsa recipes made of tomatoes and you can serve it with your meals. It will be a delicious twist in your meals.

xxxxxxxxxxxxxxxxxxxxxxxxxxxxxxxx

Recipe 13: Salsa without Onion

Cooking Time: 20 minutes

Yield: 24

List of Ingredients:

- Poblano pepper: 1
- Peeled garlic: 3 cloves
- Tomatoes: 5 ripe
- Chopped cilantro: 1 cup
- Ground cumin: 1/2 tsp.
- Chili powder: 1 tsp.
- Lime juice: 2 Tbsp.

xxxxxxxxxxxxxxxxxxxxxxxxxxxxxxxxxxxxx

Instructions:

Preheat your broiler.

Put garlic cloves and poblano pepper on a baking sheet. Turn pepper frequently and broil at a maximum distance from the heat for almost 15 minutes to make it brown.

Take one food processor and put roasted garlic, roasted pepper, lime juice, chili powder, cumin, cilantro, tomatoes in this food processor. Process with pulse setting to get a chunky texture. Chill salsa until served.

Recipe 14: Famous Salsa

Cooking Time: 10 minutes

Yield: 16

List of Ingredients:

- Stewed tomatoes: 14.5 ounce
- Diced onion: ½
- Minced garlic: 1 tsp.
- Lime: ½ (juiced)
- Salt: 1 tsp.
- Green chilies (sliced): 1/4 cup
- Fresh cilantro (chopped): 3 Tbsp.

xxxxxxxxxxxxxxxxxxxxxxxxxxxxxxxxxxx

Instructions:

Place cilantro, green chilies, salt, lime juice, garlic, onion, and tomatoes in one food processor or processor. Blend all ingredients on low to get desired consistency.

Recipe 15: Spicy Salsa

Cooking Time: 1 hour 5 minutes

Yield: 6

List of Ingredients:

- Chopped tomatoes: 4 cups
- Chopped Bell pepper (select green): 2 cups
- Chopped onion: 3/4 cup
- Jalapeno pepper: 1 cup
- Salt: 1 1/2 tsp.
- Minced garlic: 1/2 tsp.
- Cider vinegar: 1 1/4 cups

xxxxxxxxxxxxxxxxxxxxxxxxxxxxxxxxxxxxxxxx

Instructions:

Put vinegar, garlic, salt, hot pepper, onion, bell peppers and tomatoes in one pot or saucepan. Let this mixture boil and let it simmer for almost 50 – 60 minutes. Let this pasta cook longer to make it spicier.

Recipe 16: Jalapeno and Tomato Salsa

Cooking Time: 3 hours 5 minutes

Yield: 8

List of Ingredients:

- Tomatoes (peeled & sliced): 14.5 ounce
- Fresh cilantro: 1 bunch
- Minced garlic: 3 cloves
- Pepper and salt: as per taste

xxxxxxxxxxxxxxxxxxxxxxxxxxxxxxxxxxxxx

Instructions:

Take one medium bowl and mix pepper, salt, garlic, cilantro, and tomatoes in this bowl. Mix well and cover this bowl for almost three hours. Serve chilled.

Recipe 17: Habanero and Tomato Salsa

Cooking Time: 15 minutes

Yield: 24

List of Ingredients:

- Cilantro leaves: 1 bunch
- Garlic: 1 clove
- Jalapeno peppers: 2 fresh
- Diced tomatoes: 28 ounce
- Cumin: 1 tsp.
- Green onions (sliced): 4
- Lime (juiced): 1/2
- Olive oil: 1 tsp.

xxxxxxxxxxxxxxxxxxxxxxxxxxxxxxxxxxxxxxx

Instructions:

Take one food processor and add chopped cilantro, jalapeno and garlic in this processor. Add cumin and tomatoes in this food processor and coarsely chop all tomatoes.

Transfer this mixture to your bowl and stir in olive oil, lime juice and green onions. Mix well and serve chilled salsa.

Recipe 18: Mexina Salsa

Cooking Time: 40 minutes

Yield: 8

List of Ingredients:

- Green tomatoes: 3
- Jalapeno chilies (fresh): 2
- Red tomato: 1 large
- Chopped onion: 1 medium
- Lime juice: 1/4 cup
- Pepper and salt: as per taste
- Chopped cilantro: 1/2 cup

xxxxxxxxxxxxxxxxxxxxxxxxxxxxxxxxxxxxxx

Instructions:

Place jalapenos and tomatoes in one pot and cover these ingredients with water. Let this water boil to cook jalapenos and tomatoes for almost 15 minutes to turn them light green. Drain well and put in your blender with cilantro, pepper, salt, lime juice and onion. Puree all ingredients to get desired consistency, put in your fridge to serve chilled salsa.

Chapter IV - Delicious Recipes for Corn Salsa

If you love to eat corn, there are some salsa recipes to enjoy delicious and healthy salsa. These recipes are incredibly great for everyone:

Recipe 19: Corn and Tomato Salsa

Cooking Time: 30 minutes

Yield: 16

List of Ingredients:

- Corn (Whole kernel): 11 ounces
- Black olives (sliced): 4 ounces
- Roma tomatoes: 1 1/2 cups
- Red onion: 3/4 cup
- Bell pepper (seeded & diced): 1 red
- Jalapeno pepper (minced): 1 1/2 tsp.
- Avocados (pitted, peeled & diced): 1
- Olive oil: 2 Tbsp.
- Lime juice: 2 Tbsp.
- Salt: 1 tsp.

xxxxxxxxxxxxxxxxxxxxxxxxxxxxxxxxxxxxxxxx

Instructions:

Take one large bowl and mix jalapeno pepper, red pepper, onion, tomatoes, olives and corn in this bowl. Gently mix in salt, lime juice, olive oil and diced avocados.

Recipe 20: Pico de Gallo and Corn Salsa

Cooking Time: 25 minutes

Yield: 16

List of Ingredients:

- Corn kernels: 2 cups
- Red onion (diced): 1 cup
- Jicama (peeled and chopped): 2 cups
- White onion (diced): 1 cup
- Salt: 1 1/2 Tbsp.
- Red bell pepper (diced): 1 cup
- Olive oil: 1/4 cup
- White vinegar: 2 Tbsp.
- Green bell pepper (diced): 1/2 cup
- Ground cumin: 2 tsp.
- Black pepper (ground): 2 tsp.
- Red vinegar: 1 tsp.
- Chili powder: 1 tsp.
- Cilantro leaves (chopped): 2 cups
- Diced tomatoes: 1 1/2 cups
- Juiced and zested: 1 lime

xxxxxxxxxxxxxxxxxxxxxxxxxxxxxxxxxxxxxxxx

Instructions:

Heat oil in one skillet over high flame and cook corn kernel in your hot skillet. Turn frequently to avoid burning. You have to cook for almost five minutes.

Take one mixing bowl and mix corn, chili powder, red vinegar, black pepper, cumin, salt, white vinegar, olive oil, bell pepper (green) and bell pepper (red), white onion, red onion and jicama in this bowl. Add tomatoes, lime juice, lime zest and cilantro to corn mixture and stir gently to incorporate all ingredients.

Recipe 21: Black Bean Salsa with Corn

Cooking Time: 25 minutes

Yield: 72

List of Ingredients:

- Yellow corn (drained): 15 ounces
- White corn (drained) 15 ounces
- Black beans (rinsed and drained): 15 ounces
- Italian-style tomatoes (diced and drained): 14.5 ounces
- Chopped cilantro: 1 bunch
- Green onions (sliced): 5
- Chopped red onion: 1 small
- Bell pepper (seeded & chopped): 1 red
- Minced garlic: 1 Tbsp.
- Lime juice: 1/4 cup
- Diced Avocado (peeled, and pitted): 1
- Olive oil: 1 Tbsp.

xxxxxxxxxxxxxxxxxxxxxxxxxxxxxxxxxxxx

Instructions:

Stir white and yellow corn, green onion, bell pepper, garlic, red onion, cilantro, tomatoes, and black beans in one mixing bowl. Slowly mix avocado and lime juice. Drizzle with some olive oil and serve.

Recipe 22: Black Bean and Cheese Salsa

Cooking Time: 30 minutes

Yield: 10

List of Ingredients:

- Corn (cleaned and husked): 1 ear
- Black beans (reduced sodium): 15 ounces
- Cottage cheese: 32 ounces
- Avocado (pitted and peeled): 1
- Roma tomatoes/plum tomatoes (diced and seeded): 2
- Salsa: 2 cups
- Tortilla chips: 13.5 ounces

xxxxxxxxxxxxxxxxxxxxxxxxxxxxxxxxxxxxxxxxx

Instructions:

Put corn with cob in your microwave-safe dish with almost ¼-inch water. Cover this dish and microwaves on medium-high for almost four minutes to tender corn. Keep corns under running water to make them cool and make slices of kernels from its cob, keep it aside.

You can use one small saucepan and cook black beans in this pan for almost 10 minutes to tender. Strain beans and rinse under running/cold water to remove extra sodium and liquid. Keep it aside.

Add cotton cheese in serving bowl, peel and dice avocado in small pieces. Add corn, salsa black beans and cottage cheese in saucepan. Stir well and put in your fridge until you are ready to serve. You can serve with some tortilla chips.

Recipe 23: Roasted and Chipotle Salsa with Corn

Cooking Time: 25 minutes

Yield: 20

List of Ingredients:

- Frozen corn: 2 cups
- Vine-ripened tomatoes (chopped in ½-inch pieces): 2
- Diced red onion: 1 small
- Diced bell pepper (red color): 3/4 cup
- Jalapeno peppers (remove seeds): 2
- Chopped chipotle pepper: 2 tsp.
- Lime juice: 4 Tbsp.
- Olive oil: 1 Tbsp.
- Chopped cilantro: ¼ cup
- Cooking spray: as per your needs
- Salt: as per taste

xxxxxxxxxxxxxxxxxxxxxxxxxxxxxxxxxxxxxx

Instructions:

Grease one nonstick skillet with cooking spray and put over medium flame. Add corn in skillet and cook well to avoid burning and allow them to become browned. Put in one large bowl.

Stir jalapeno peppers, bell pepper, onion and tomatoes in corn and sprinkle some reserved seeds of jalapeno. Mix in chipotle pepper, cilantro, olive oil and lime juice. Season salsa with salt as per your taste.

Recipe 24: Corn Salad with Cilantro

Cooking Time: 55 minutes

Yield: 6

List of Ingredients:

- Corn on cob (remove husks and silk removed): 2 ears
- Chopped tomatoes: 2
- Avocados (peeled, pitted & diced): 2
- Cilantro (cut off stems and chop leaves): 1/2 bunch
- Chopped white onion: 1
- Chopped garlic: 3 Tbsp.
- Olive oil: 2 Tbsp.
- Red vinegar: 2 Tbsp.
- Salt: as per your taste

xxxxxxxxxxxxxxxxxxxxxxxxxxxxxxxxxxxxx

Instructions:

Preheat your grill to almost medium heat and lightly grease your grate. Cook corn on your preheated grill for approximately 3 – 5 minutes. Try to turn them often to avoid burning.

Cut off the kernel cobs, make sure to transfer in a large salad bowl. Stir in red vinegar, olive oil, white onion, garlic, cilantro, avocados, and tomatoes.

Chapter V - Mango and Peach Salsa Recipes

For delicious salsa with peach and mangoes, you can get the advantage of these recipes. You can try these recipes to make delicious salsa with fruity flavors:

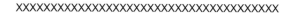

Recipe 25: Chipotle Peach Salsa

Cooking Time: 40 minutes

Yield: 12

List of Ingredients:

- Balsamic vinegar: 2 Tbsp.
- Orange juice: 2/3 cup
- Lemon juice: 1/4 cup
- Lime juice: 2 Tbsp.
- Diced mango: 2
- Diced strawberries: 2 pints

xxxxxxxxxxxxxxxxxxxxxxxxxxxxxxxxxxxxxxxx

Instructions:

Stir lime juice, orange juice, balsamic vinegar and lemon juice in one bowl. Gently fold strawberries and mangoes in lemon juice mixture and keep this mixture aside for almost 20 minutes. Serve chilled.

Recipe 26: Peach Salsa with Cinnamon Chips

Cooking Time: 30 minutes

Yield: 8

List of Ingredients:

Salsa:

- Diced Peaches (pitted and peeled): 8
- Cherry tomatoes in Yellow Color (quartered): 1/2 cup
- Chopped red onion: 1/4
- Chopped cilantro: 2 Tbsp.
- Jalapeno pepper (seeded and discard membrane): ½
- Chopped pepper: ½
- Ground cardamom: 1/4 tsp.
- Lime (juiced): 1
- Lemon juice: 1 Tbsp.

Chips:

- Flour tortillas (8 wedges): 10 small
- Melted Butter: 1/4 cup
- Cinnamon sugar: 2 Tbsp.

xxxxxxxxxxxxxxxxxxxxxxxxxxxxxxxxxxxxx

Instructions:

Mix jalapeno pepper, cilantro, onion, tomatoes, and peaches in one bowl. Sprinkle with some cardamom and pour lemon juice and lime juice over salsa. Toss well to coat.

Preheat your oven to nearly 350° F.

Carefully brush all tortilla wedges with some melted butter and generously sprinkle with cinnamon sugar. Now arrange all coated wedges on one baking sheet.

Bake in your preheated oven for almost 15 minutes to make chips crispy. You can serve crispy chips with peach salsa.

Recipe 27: Peachanero Salsa

Cooking Time: 8 hours 30 minutes

Yield: 40

List of Ingredients:

- Diced peaches: 8 ounces
- Chopped peach: 1 firm
- Chopped red onion: 1
- Habanero peppers (seeded & minced): 2
- Minced cilantro: 8 sprigs
- Lime juice (fresh): 2 Tbsp.
- Tequila: 1/4 cup
- Olive oil (extra-virgin): 2 Tbsp.
- Black pepper (ground) and salt: as per taste

xxxxxxxxxxxxxxxxxxxxxxxxxxxxxxxxxxx

Instructions:

Toss cilantro, habanero pepper, onion, chopped peach and canned peaches in one mixing bowl. Pour olive oil, tequila, and lime juice in this bowl and mix all ingredients well. Season with pepper and salt, cover this bowl and put in your fridge for almost eight hours to serve chilled.

Recipe 28: Mango Salsa

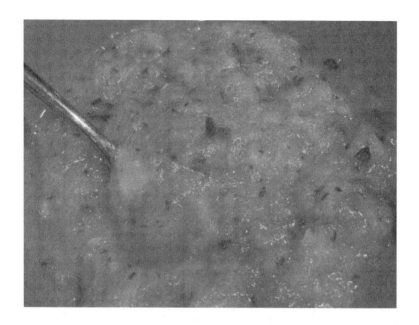

Cooking Time: 40 minutes

Yield: 24

List of Ingredients:

- Halved and peeled onion: 1 red
- Diced Mangos (peeled & seeded): 12
- Pressed garlic: 1/2 head
- Habanero peppers (seeded & minced): 3
- Chopped fresh cilantro: 1 bunch
- Apple cider vinegar: 2 Tbsp.
- Salt: as per taste

xxxxxxxxxxxxxxxxxxxxxxxxxxxxxxxxxxxxxx

Instructions:

Preheat your outdoor grill for nearly high heat. Lightly grease your grill grate and put onion on the grill. Cook to make it slightly black.

Chop onion and combine them with apple cider, cilantro, habanero, garlic and mango in one mixing bowl. Sprinkle with some salt as per taste. Serve this delicious salsa.

Recipe 29: Apple and Peach Salsa

Cooking Time: 3 hours 20 minutes

Yield: 6

List of Ingredients:

- Diced peaches: 1 cup
- Diced apple: 1/2 cup
- Diced avocado: 1/2 cup
- Diced tomato: 1/2 cup
- Green onion (Chopped): 1/3 cup
- Chopped cilantro: 1/4 cup
- Lemon juice: 2 Tbsp.
- Olive oil: 2 Tbsp.
- Sesame oil (toasted): 1 tsp.
- Ground cumin: 1 tsp.
- Jalapeno pepper (seeded & minced): 1
- Black pepper (ground) and salt: as per taste

xxxxxxxxxxxxxxxxxxxxxxxxxxxxxxxxxxx

Instructions:

Take one bowl and mix jalapeno pepper, black pepper, salt, cumin, sesame oil, olive oil, lemon juice, cilantro, green onion, tomato, avocado, apple and peaches in this bowl.

Cover this bowl with one plastic wrap and put in your fridge for almost three hours to blend all flavors. Serve this salsa chilled.

Recipe 30: Peach and Pineapple Salsa

Cooking Time: 1 hour 20 minutes

Yield: 16

List of Ingredients:

- Chopped mangos (peeled and seeded): 2
- Small peaches (halved & pitted): 2 (1/2-inch dice pieces)
- Diced pineapple: 1 cup
- Chopped tomatoes: 4
- Diced white onion: 1
- Diced red bell pepper: 1
- Diced bell pepper (yellow): 1
- Chopped cilantro: 1 cup
- Minced garlic: 1 clove
- Minced jalapeno pepper: 1 small
- Lime juice: 2 Tbsp.
- Salt: 1 tsp.
- White sugar: 2 Tbsp.
- Water: 3/4 cup

xxxxxxxxxxxxxxxxxxxxxxxxxxxxxxxxxxxxxx

Instructions:

Put cilantro, yellow pepper, red pepper, onion, tomato, pineapple, peach and mango in one mixing bowl. Mix in the water, sugar, salt, lime juice, jalapeno, and garlic.

Cover this bowl and put in the fridge for almost one hour to serve chilled salsa.

About the Author

Heston Brown is an accomplished chef and successful e-book author from Palo Alto California. After studying cooking at The New England Culinary Institute, Heston stopped briefly in Chicago where he was offered head chef at some of the city's most prestigious restaurants. Brown decide that he missed the rolling hills and sunny weather of California and moved back to his home state to open up his own catering company and give private cooking classes.

Heston lives in California with his beautiful wife of 18 years and his two daughters who also have aspirations to follow in their father's footsteps and pursue careers in the culinary arts. Brown is well known for his delicious fish and chicken dishes and teaches these recipes as well as many others to his students.

When Heston gave up his successful chef position in Chicago and moved back to California, a friend suggested he use the internet to share his recipes with the world and so he did! To date, Heston Brown has written over 1000 e-books that contain recipes, cooking tips, business strategies for catering companies and a self-help book he wrote from personal experience.

He claims his wife has been his inspiration throughout many of his endeavours and continues to be his partner in business as well as life. His greatest joy is having all three women in his life in the kitchen with him cooking their favourite meal while his favourite jazz music plays in the background.

Author's Afterthoughts

Thank you to all the readers who invested time and money into my book! I cherish every one of you and hope you took the same pleasure in reading it as I did in writing it.

Out of all of the books out there, you chose mine and for that I am truly grateful. It makes the effort worth it when I know my readers are enjoying my work from beginning to end.

Please take a few minutes to write an Amazon review so that others can benefit from your opinions and insight. Your review will help countless other readers make an informed choice

Thank you so much,

Heston Brown

Made in the USA
Columbia, SC
10 August 2022